Taylor Swift
From Little Star to Superstar

Chasing Dreams and Catching Stars

By Harmony A. Star

Illustrated by Lily Thompson

The author dedicates this book to all children, wherever you may be.

This is for you, the dreamers, the believers, the star chasers and the melody makers. Just like the little girl with golden hair and bright blue eyes called Taylor Swift, you too have the power to turn your dreams into beautiful reality.

Remember, every dream you hold is a melody waiting to be sung. Every star you reach for is a dream waiting to be realized. And every story you write is a chapter in the unique song of your life.

So, dream big, sing loud and keep chasing those stars.

And, most importantly, remember this - just like Taylor, you are capable of turning your own big dreams into reality.

Your story is just beginning and I can't wait to see where your dreams take you.

With all my heart,
Harmony A. Star

Introduction

"Did you ever dream about being a star? Imagine a world where every thought you have turns into a beautiful song!"

"In a cosy little town named Reading, there lived a little girl with golden hair and bright blue eyes. Her name was Taylor Alison Swift. At bedtime, instead of fairy tales, Taylor dreamed of melodies."

"With a heart full of dreams and her head filled with songs, Taylor wished upon every star to sing her stories to the world. Just like the way birds spread their wings and fly, she wanted her music to fly far and wide, touching the hearts of everyone who heard it."

"Come, let's turn the pages and sing along with the magical journey of Taylor Swift, a little girl who dreamed big and became a superstar, reminding all of us to dream a little dream every day!"

This Book Belongs To:

_____

Chapter One
Little Taylor's Big Dreams

In the quiet town of Reading, nestled between the hills and trees, was the Swift family home. Inside, a little girl named Taylor was about to discover a love that would change her life forever.

Do you have something you love so much that you can spend the whole day doing it? For Taylor, that was music. She would sway to the rhythm of the wind, tap her tiny toes to the pitter-patter of raindrops and hum along with the chirping birds.

Every night, as the stars began to twinkle, Taylor would lie in bed listening to her Mum read her a bedtime story. She loved the characters, the adventures and the magic. But Taylor didn't just want to hear stories, she wanted to tell them. And she wanted to tell them with music!

One day, a big box arrived at the Swift house. Can you guess what was inside? A guitar! But this was no small guitar, it was almost as tall as Taylor. It was love at first strum. Even though her fingers were small and the strings were tough, Taylor would not be stopped.

Every day after school, Taylor would rush home, do her homework and then pick up her big guitar. She would practice and practice, even when her fingers hurt, even when the chords were tough. Because when she played, she felt like she could touch the stars.

"Strum, strum, strum," went her guitar. Each strum told a story, each strum was a step closer to her dream. Can you hear it? That's the sound of little Taylor's big dreams beginning to take flight!

I hope this offers an exciting picture of Taylor's early interest in music and her determination to master the guitar.

Chapter Two
Taylor's Tiny Triumphs

Once upon a time, in a little girl's heart, big dreams started to grow. This little girl was Taylor, and she had a secret. Want to know what it was? She had begun to write songs!

Did you know that words can dance and play just like we do? Taylor knew! She made words twirl and spin into songs, songs that told stories about her dreams, her friends and her little world.

One day, Taylor did something truly amazing. She wrote a poem, a poem so beautiful that it won a big prize! This made Taylor's heart glow with happiness. She thought, "If I can make words dance in a poem, I can make them sing in a song!"

And that's just what she did. Taylor's songs started to fill up every room in her house, then every street in her town and soon, she was ready for an even bigger adventure.

With her family by her side, Taylor moved to a faraway city called Nashville. It was a place where songs grow like beautiful flowers, a place where Taylor could share her songs with the world.

There were many famous musical artists there and she met people who loved her songs as much as she did. They said, "Taylor, your songs are special. Let's share them with everyone!" And so, Taylor signed her first record deal. Her dreams were starting to come true!

Did Taylor stop dreaming then? Oh no! Each little win made her dream bigger, try harder and believe in her music even more. She knew this was just the beginning and she was ready to reach for the stars!

Chapter Three
Taylor's Musical Magic

In this bustling city called Nashville, Taylor was about to sprinkle some magic. Not with a magic wand, but with her songs. She strummed her guitar, sang from her heart and something extraordinary began to happen.

Her first song was called "Tim McGraw." It was not about a farmer or a cowboy, but about feelings and memories. When people heard it, they started to smile, remembering their own special moments.

Next came an album, an album as shiny as a treasure chest, full of enchanting songs. She named it "Taylor Swift," just like her name. Can you guess what happened? It soared up, up, up the music charts, just like a bird soaring in the sky!

Then Taylor decided to create more magic. She created an album named "Fearless," and it was full of brave and beautiful songs. People everywhere loved it! They laughed, cried and danced to Taylor's music. It filled hearts and souls in every corner of the world.

Have you ever seen a shooting star? Taylor's music was like a shooting star, lighting up the sky, dazzling everyone who saw it. More albums followed, like "Speak Now," "Red," and "1989." Each album was a new magical journey, full of stories that everyone loved.

Just like a rainbow after a rainy day, Taylor's music brought joy and colour into people's lives. Her songs were like best friends, always there to make you feel happy, understood and cared for. From the little town of Reading to the big city of Nashville, Taylor's music had become magic that echoed around the world!

Chapter Four
Taylor's Brave Adventures

Do you remember the story of the Little Engine That Could? Just like that tiny, determined engine, our friend Taylor faced some big mountains on her journey to stardom.

One of the tallest mountains was when Taylor decided to change her music. For a long time, she had been making country music, like the songs you'd hear on a farm with cows and chickens. But then, Taylor decided to try something new. She wanted to make pop music, like the catchy tunes you'd hear at a fun, bouncy party or on the radio.

People were surprised. They said, "Taylor, we love your country songs. Can you make pop music that we will love just as much?" Taylor was nervous, but she truly believed in herself. She took a deep breath, strummed her guitar and started to climb that mountain.

Up, up, up she climbed, making pop music that was as sparkly and fun as a box of glitter. People heard her new music, and guess what? They loved it! They danced, they clapped and they sang along. Taylor had reached the top of the mountain and showed everyone that she could make magical music, no matter the genre!

But her journey didn't stop there. Sometimes, people would say unkind things about Taylor's music. But do you know what Taylor did? She remembered the wise words of her mum, "Taylor, not everyone has to like everything you do. What matters is that you love what you do."

And so, Taylor kept going. She didn't let the unkind words stop her. Instead, she used them to make her stronger. Like a brave explorer, she used every challenge as a steppingstone and every setback as a lesson. Because Taylor knew that being brave wasn't about never being scared, but about not letting fear stop you from following your dreams.

Chapter Five
Taylor's Shiny Trophies

Imagine a night sky full of twinkling stars. Now, imagine if you could reach out and grab one of those stars. That's what it felt like when Taylor won her very first Grammy award!

What's a Grammy, you ask? It's a shiny golden trophy that says, "Well done, you've made amazing music!" It's one of the biggest prizes a musician can win. And Taylor, our brave adventurer, won not just one Grammy, but many!

One of her special albums, "Fearless," made everyone sit up and take notice. It won the Album of the Year Grammy, making Taylor the youngest person to win this big award! Can you imagine the joy in her heart holding that golden trophy?

But that's not all! Taylor's songs reached so far and wide that they landed in millions of hearts around the world. This made her one of the best-selling music artists of all time! That's like having her music in almost every home, making people dance, laugh, sing along and feel great.

From the little girl who dreamed of making music in Reading, to the superstar whose songs echoed around the world, Taylor had truly made her mark. She showed us that with courage, love for what we do and a heart full of dreams we can all touch the stars!

Just like the stars in the sky, Taylor's shiny trophies are reminders of her journey, her music and her dreams. They sparkle with all the hard work, love and magic she put into her songs.

Chapter Six
Taylor's Heart of Gold

You know how a candle lights up a room? Taylor decided to do the same with her love. She had a heart as big as her music and she wanted to share it with the world. Just as her songs brought joy, Taylor wanted to bring help and hope to those in need.

Remember the magic of Taylor's music? She decided to sprinkle that magic in places where it was needed most. When people were sad or in trouble, Taylor was there to help. She gave away lots of money to people who needed it, like a fairy spreading joy with her magic wand.

Once, when many homes were destroyed by a big, scary storm, Taylor gave a million dollars to help people rebuild their houses and their lives. Can you imagine how happy and relieved those people felt? Taylor had turned her musical magic into helping magic!

But Taylor didn't stop there. She also believed in standing up for what's right, just like a brave knight from a storybook. She spoke out when she saw something wrong and worked to change it. Whether it was making sure other artists got paid fairly for their music or standing up for people who were being treated badly, Taylor was there.

Just like in her songs, Taylor showed that everyone can make a difference. By helping others and standing up for what's right, we can all be heroes in our own way.

With her heart of gold, Taylor showed us that the true magic of being a star is not only in creating beautiful music but also in helping others and making the world a brighter place.

Chapter Seven
Taylor's Song of Dreams

From the little girl with a big dream in Reading, to a superstar whose music filled hearts around the world, our friend Taylor has taken us on a magical journey.

Remember how Taylor wrote songs that made us laugh, cry, and dance? She taught us that it's okay to dream big, just like she did. Dreams, after all, are like seeds. When we care for them, they can grow into something beautiful.

And you know what's even more special? Taylor showed us that everyone has their own song to sing, their own story to tell. Just like how she shared her stories through her music, we can share our own stories, in our own special way.

We learned from Taylor that it's okay to be different. Whether it's trying new things like changing the type of music we make, or standing up for what we believe in, it's all a part of who we are. Taylor's journey shows us that being brave is about being ourselves and shining our own light.

Remember when Taylor helped people in need and stood up for what was right? She showed us that sharing our sparkle with the world can make it a better place. Just like Taylor, we can give kindness and love to those around us.

Taylor's melody continues to shine, encouraging us to dance to our own tunes. Each one of us is unique, like a special note in a beautiful song. And when we believe in ourselves, we can create our own magical music.

So, what's your dream? What's your song? Remember, just like Taylor, you can touch the stars and fill the world with your own special magic.

"Dream Big, Sing Loud"

(Verse 1)

"In a town called Reading, under the bright blue sky,

Lived a little girl named Taylor, with dreams that fly high.

She strummed on her guitar, both night and day,

Singing her heart out, in her own special way.

(Chorus)

Dream big, dream high, let your spirit fly,

Just like Taylor, under the wide-open sky.

Dance to your own beat, sing your own song,

Believe in your dreams and you'll never go wrong.

(Verse 2)

She sang about love, she sang about life,

About being brave, through life's joy and strife.

Her words touched hearts, both near and far,

Showing us all, we can all be a star.

(Chorus)

Dream big, dream high, let your spirit fly,

Just like Taylor, under the wide-open sky.

Dance to your own beat, sing your own song,

Believe in your dreams and you'll never go wrong.

(Bridge)

From a little town girl to a star so bright,

Taylor shows us to hold our dreams tight.

With love in our hearts and a story to share,

Just like Taylor we can sparkle anywhere.

(Chorus)

Dream big, dream high, let your spirit fly,

Just like Taylor, under the wide-open sky.

Dance to your own beat, sing your own song,

Believe in your dreams, you're brave and strong.

(Outro)

So, here's to you, and to Taylor's song,

Keep dreaming, keep singing, all day long.

In every heart, there's a story to tell,

So, let's sing it out loud, and let's sing it well."

20 fun facts about
Taylor Swift

1. Christmas Baby: Taylor Swift was born on December 13, 1989. Her birthday falls very close to Christmas, which is fitting because she loves the holiday season.

2. Name Inspiration: Her mother named her after the singer James Taylor in the hopes that it would give her a business advantage if she became successful.

3. Young Poet: When she was in fourth grade, Taylor won a national poetry contest with a poem called "Monster in My Closet."

4. Musical Start: She learned to play guitar after a computer repairman showed her a few chords when he came to her house to fix her computer.

5. Young Songwriter: Swift wrote her first song, "Lucky You," when she was only 12.

6. Swift Move: Her family moved to Nashville when she was 14 to help her break into country music.

7. First Album: Her first album was released when she was 16 and went triple platinum.

8. Young Achiever: She is the youngest artist to write and perform a number one song on the Hot Country Songs chart.

9. Fear of Sea Creatures: Taylor has a fear of sea urchins, calling them "a grenade" that could go off at any time.

10. Guinness World Record: She holds several Guinness World Records, including Fastest Selling Digital Album by a Female Artist for "folklore."

11. Cat Lover: She adores cats and has three of her own named Meredith Grey, Olivia Benson and Benjamin Button, named after her favourite TV characters.

12. Acting Debut: Taylor made her acting debut in an episode of CSI: Crime Scene Investigation in 2009.

13. Favourite Number: Her favourite number is 13 and she considers it her lucky number.

14. Album Routine: She releases her albums every other year in the autumn, a pattern that continued until her album "Lover," released in the summer of 2019.

15. Real Estate Investor: Taylor owns real estate in Nashville, Los Angeles, New York City and Rhode Island.

16. Surprise Songs: She often performs a surprise, unannounced song for fans during her concerts.

17. Fear of Tattoos: She has said that she is afraid of getting a tattoo because she fears it may not remain significant to her in the future.

18. Starbucks Lovers: In her song "Blank Space," the line that sounds like "Starbucks lovers" is actually "got a long list of ex-lovers."

19. Secret Messages: In the lyric booklets of her early albums, she capitalized certain letters that spelled out hidden messages.

20. Famous Friends: Her group of friends includes many well-known celebrities, such as Selena Gomez, Ed Sheeran and the members of the band HAIM.

25 Milestones that
Define Taylor Swift's
Remarkable Career Journey

1. Imagine this, Taylor became the youngest person to write songs for a big music company.

2. She climbed to the top of the country music chart with a song she wrote herself, like winning a big game of musical hide-and-seek.

3. Her second album, "Fearless," was like a magical key that opened the door to the Best Album of the Year award.

4. Just like a musical superhero, Taylor also won the Best Album of the Year award twice.

5. In 2019, they even called her the Artist of the Decade, a pretty long time to be making such wonderful music at such a young age.

6. Taylor was named the Best Musician of the Year twice, just like being the star player of the year in a big musical sports team.

7. Four of her albums sold over a million copies in just one week. Imagine all those CDs stacked up!

8. Taylor got a star with her name on it in the famous Hollywood Walk of Fame in 2019, a bit like a golden treasure map with her name as the "X" marking the spot.

9. Taylor created a fun app that was so popular it won an Emmy award so she had built a digital playground that everyone wanted to play in.

10. Taylor surprised everyone by making two albums, "Folklore" and "Evermore," like hidden gifts that everyone found and loved.

11. Taylor has won so many American Music Awards, it's almost like she's collecting musical trophies.

12. In the world of Country Music, Taylor has won 11 awards, including a very special award, like a shiny musical medal.

13. Taylor won 28 Billboard Music Awards, like having a trophy for every day of the month, and then some.

14. One time, she was given an award with her very own name on it, a special honour indeed.

15. Some of Taylor's songs reached the top of the charts, like musical mountaineers.

16. Taylor won 10 Grammy Awards, like winning the gold medal in the musical Olympics.

17. Taylor's music video for her song "You Need to Calm Down" was chosen as the best of the year.

18. Her "Red" album has the record for the most simultaneous U.S. Hot 100 entries by a female artist.

19. "1989" was one of the best-selling albums of the decade, marking her transition from country to pop music.

20. Taylor was named a Global Icon at the 2021 BRIT Awards.

21. She made it to Time's 100 most influential people list three times.

22. At the 2022 American Music Awards, she was named Artist of the Year and Favourite Country Female Artist.

23. The 2022 Billboard Music Awards honoured her as Top Billboard 200 Artist, Top Country Artist, Top Country Female Artist and also gave her the Top Country Album award for 'Red (Taylor's Version).

24. At the 2023 Grammy Awards, she won the Best Music Video for 'All Too Well: The Short Film'.

25. Taylor has broken 92 Guinness World Records, which is quite an achievement in itself. (As of 6th Jan 2023)

DIGIDOG

"Unleash Your Curiosity: Discovering the World - A DigiDog Series of Books in Honour of Chico, Our Beloved Pomeranian"

Welcome to a new series of books, crafted in memory of our dear pet Pomeranian called Chico. For over 15 years, he continued to delight us with his never-ending curiosity, constantly exploring and investigating everything, everywhere he went.

It is in honour of his spirit of exploration that we present this exciting collection of books that we hope will quench your thirst for knowledge and spark your imagination.

In the series, you will embark on a journey of fascinating people with unique life stories, intriguing subjects and the mysteries of the world. Each book provides a number of carefully researched and thoughtfully curated facts that are designed to surprise, enlighten and entertain you.

From the depths of the ocean to the heights of the sky and beyond, our books will transport you to new worlds and reveal the wonders that lie within them. Join us on this adventure and let Chico's legacy inspire you to never stop exploring and learning.

The DigiDog series includes books for both children and adults.

END

Thank you!

Hey, little superstar! We've reached the end of our magical journey with Taylor Swift. Wasn't it fun to dance along with her songs and dream big with her stories?

We hope you enjoyed this book as much as we enjoyed creating it for you. The words and the colourful pictures were made with lots of love just for you! From the little star in Reading to the superstar touching hearts around the world, we travelled with Taylor and learned about dreams, bravery, and sharing our sparkle.

Remember all the pretty pictures that brought Taylor's story to life? Weren't they as sparkly and fun as a box of glitter? We hope they made you smile, laugh and dream along with Taylor.

Thank you so much for reading this book. Your journey with Taylor might be over, but your own magical adventure is just beginning! Keep dreaming and keep being your own amazing self. And remember, you too can touch the stars and fill the world with your own special magic.

Name : Harmony A. Star

Harmony A Star

Position : Editor

Lorean Publishing House – a DigiDog Discovers book.

BONUS CONTENT: A Colorful Journey with Taylor!

Get ready to add a splash of color to the world of Taylor Swift! At the end of this book, we've included a special treat for all you creative souls. Dive into 10 exclusive coloring pages, each capturing an iconic moment of Taylor's illustrious journey. Whether you're a budding artist or just looking for a relaxing escape, these pages offer a unique way to connect with Taylor's world. So, grab your favorite colors and let's bring Taylor's magic to life, one page at a time!

Printed in the USA
CPSIA information can be obtained
at www.ICGtesting.com
LVHW080850101123
763485LV00084B/2986